Focus

The focus of this book is:

- to read to understand a concept,
- to use new, technical vocabulary.

Tuning In

The front cover

Let's read the title together.

Speaking and Listening

Discuss the front cover. Explain that this is a non-fiction book with a photograph on the cover, rather than an illustration.

What do you think a seedling is?

Let's look in the index on page 16. What pages should we look at to find 'seedling'?

Where is 'seedling' on page 9?

Where is it on page 11?

What is a seedling?

The back cover

Let's read the blurb on the back cover to find out what this book is about. Discuss how this non-fiction book might differ from a fiction one.

Title page

Read the title again.

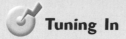

Tuning In

Where is the pine tree growing?

Observe and Prompt

Word Recognition

- Check the children can read the word 'pine' using their decoding skills. Help them with the vowel sound (from 'i' and silent 'e') if they struggle.

- Check the children can read 'tree', 'grows', 'strong' and 'from' blending the adjacent consonants at the beginning of these words, and then blending through the whole of each word from left to right.

A pine tree grows tall and strong.
Where did it come from?

3

Language Comprehension

- Check the children are using the punctuation to read with appropriate intonation.
- Ask the children what type of tree this is.
- Ask the children where they think the tree came from.

3

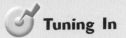

Tuning In

Where do you think the pine cone grows?

Observe and Prompt

Word Recognition

- Check the children can read the word 'tiny' using their decoding skills. Help them with the long 'i' sound if they struggle.

- If the children have difficulty reading 'inside', prompt them to break the word down into two syllables, – 'in' and 'side', before blending the word together from left to right.

- If the children have difficulty with the word 'cone', help them with the vowel sound (from 'o' and silent 'e').

A pine tree comes from a tiny
seed inside a pine cone.
Pine cones grow on pine trees.

5

Language Comprehension

- Check the children understand where the pine tree comes from.
- Ask the children what is inside a pine cone.
- Ask the children where pine cones grow.

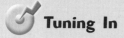 **Tuning In**

What do you think happens to the pine cones?

What might happen to the seeds?

 Observe and Prompt

Word Recognition

- If the children have difficulty with the word 'fall', help them with the vowel sound in this word.

- Check the children can read 'ground' using their decoding skills. Can they read the adjacent consonants in this word?

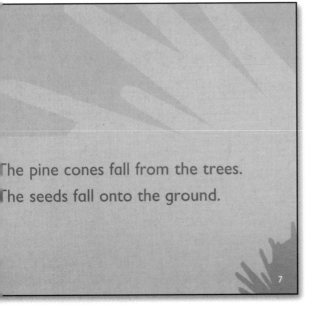

The pine cones fall from the trees.
The seeds fall onto the ground.

7

Language Comprehension

- Check that the children are reading fluently with appropriate phrasing.
- Ask the children what happens to the pine cones.
- What do the children think happens to the seeds inside the cones?

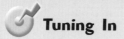

Tuning In

What do you think the seeds grow into?

seed

Observe and Prompt

Word Recognition

- If the children have difficulty with the word 'Each', model the reading of this word for them.

- If the children have difficulty with the word 'seedling', prompt them to break it down into two syllables – 'seed' and 'ling', before blending the whole word together from left to right.

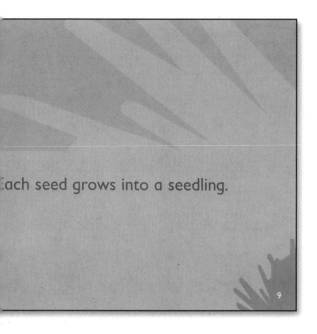

Each seed grows into a seedling.

9

Language Comprehension

- Ask the children what happens to each seedling.
- Ask the children what the arrow on the picture shows.
- What do the children think will happen to the seedling?

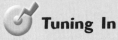 **Tuning In**

What do you think the seedling is doing on this page?

Speaking and Listening

Can you see the three dots at the end of the words?

What are they for?

 Observe and Prompt

Word Recognition

- Check the children are reading the words 'seedling' and 'grows' more confidently using their decoding skills.

The seedling grows and grows . . .

11

👁 Observe and Prompt

Language Comprehension

- Check that the children understand the purpose of the dots (*ellipsis*) and can make a quick page turn.
- Ask the children what they think the seedling will become?

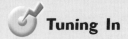 **Tuning In**

What do you think the seedling has grown into?

Observe and Prompt

Word Recognition

- Check the children can read 'little' using their decoding skills. Help them with the 'le' sound if this phoneme has not yet been taught.
- If the children have difficulty with the word 'called', model the blending of this word for them.
- If the children have difficulty with the word 'sapling', prompt them to break the word down into two syllables – 'sap' and 'ling', before blending the whole word together.

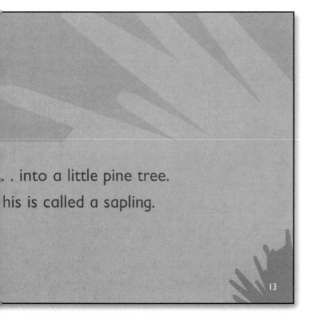

. . . into a little pine tree.
his is called a sapling.

13

 Observe and Prompt

Language Comprehension

- Check that the children are reading with appropriate phrasing, observing punctuation.
- Ask the children what the little pine tree is called.
- What do the children think the sapling will grow into?

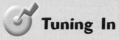

Tuning In

What do you think the sapling has grown into?

What might grow on the big, strong pine tree?

 Observe and Prompt

Word Recognition

- Check the children are using their decoding skills more confidently to read 'strong', 'grow' and 'tree'.

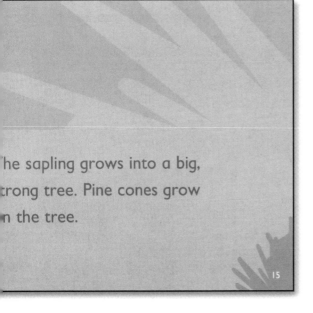

he sapling grows into a big,
trong tree. Pine cones grow
n the tree.

15

 Observe and Prompt

Language Comprehension

- Ask the children what the sapling grows into.
- Ask the children what grows on the pine tree.
- Check the children understand that we have gone round in a circle.
- Have the children ever grown anything from seed?

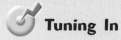

Tuning In

This page is the index page.

Speaking and Listening

How would you use an index page?

> **Index**
>
> pine cone 5, 7, 15
> pine tree 3, 5, 13
> sapling 13, 15
> seedling 9, 11
> seeds 5, 7, 8, 9
>
> 16

 Observe and Prompt

Word Recognition

- Check the children can read all the words in the index using their decoding skills.

Language Comprehension

- Check the children understand the purpose of the index.
- Ask the children where they would look to find information about a 'seedling'. Ask them to check the pages.